Not Only the Extraordinary
are Entering the Dream World

# NOT ONLY THE EXTRAORDINARY ARE ENTERING THE DREAM WORLD

Martin Willitts Jr.

Flowstone Press

Not Only the Extraordinary
are Entering the Dream World

Copyright © 2022 Martin Willitts Jr.
Cover image "Fifth World" © 2022 Michael Spring

First Flowstone Press Edition • November 2022
ISBN 978-1-945824-61-6

Flowstone Press,
an Imprint of Left Fork
www.leftforkbooks.com

# TABLE OF CONTENTS

## I. THE JOURNEY

| | |
|---|---|
| Dawn | 3 |
| The Organ Mountain Range | 4 |
| At Mountain Crest | 7 |
| Teenagers Hiking in the Forest | 9 |
| Exploring the Mountain Range | 10 |
| Camping | 13 |
| Snake River | 15 |
| From the Closeness of Oak, Where Dark Holds Breath | 21 |
| Heat Index Breaks the Temperature Gauge | 22 |
| Dry Spell | 23 |
| Third Warning | 24 |
| It Is Drizzling Heat | 25 |
| Extreme Heat | 26 |
| Rain Patterns | 27 |
| Inexplicable Rain | 28 |
| The Absence of a Lake | 29 |
| Water Music | 30 |
| The Day They Stole the Water | 32 |
| Wind Shear | 33 |
| Survival Depends Upon Your Definition of Recovery | 34 |
| There is Darkness to the Water | 35 |
| Rowing | 36 |
| March | 37 |
| Releasing the Dark Landscape | 38 |
| Clear-Cut | 40 |
| The Glass-Faced Deer of Boonville, New York | 41 |
| The Lilac Bushes and the Forest-Tent Caterpillars | 42 |
| Silk Worms | 44 |
| The Wire Fence Holding Back the World | 45 |

| | |
|---|---:|
| What I Want | 47 |
| Loss | 50 |
| *Above the Spring Tâf* | 51 |
| Forest | 52 |
| In the High Hills | 53 |
| *Below the Beech, Above the Tâf* | 54 |
| Morning | 55 |
| Spring | 56 |
| Defeated | 57 |
| Speaking the Language of Deer | 58 |
| Lost | 60 |

## II. LOVE IS A JOURNEY

| | |
|---|---:|
| How to Find Love | 65 |
| Some Things You Can Never Repair | 67 |
| I Cannot Stop Pain | 68 |
| Why Darkness Whimpers | 69 |
| Van Gogh's *Starry Night* | 70 |
| First Spring Morning | 71 |
| Listening into the Silence | 72 |
| Twenty Reasons | 73 |
| The Gifts | 74 |
| Six Love Poems | 75 |
| Day Lilies | 78 |
| An Exaltation of Larks | 79 |
| The Moment Stillness Moves | 80 |
| Longing Is Like the Seed | 81 |
| At the End of the Day | 82 |
| After Service | 83 |
| Miracles Are a Dime a Dozen | 84 |
| Clear for Miles and Miles | 85 |
| Hatching | 86 |

## III. MEDITATION AS A JOURNEY

| | |
|---|---|
| Walking Hill Slopes | 91 |
| The Bird Count | 92 |
| Nighttime | 93 |
| Argument | 94 |
| Someday the World Will Shudder like This | 95 |
| On a Rainy Day | 96 |
| Tanka | 97 |
| Revitalizing | 98 |
| When Light Reaches Us | 99 |
| Pacific Treefrog | 101 |
| The Clearing | 104 |
| In the Woods | 105 |
| Quickening | 106 |
| Sensing in the Darkness | 107 |
| Beyond Sight | 108 |
| Of Momentary Breaths None of Us Could Ever Recover | 109 |
| We Live Within Expandable Music | 110 |
| Fall | 111 |
| Fall Message | 112 |
| Five Untitled Short Poems | 114 |
| Come Through the Waist-High Ferns | 116 |
| Observation | 117 |
| The Nightingale Only Sings at Sunset | 118 |
| I Didn't Know What to Say | 119 |
| Now | 121 |
| Folding | 122 |
| Paddling | 123 |
| How to Know Love # 2 | 124 |
| Maple Leaf Wings | 125 |
| Eventually | 126 |
| The Way | 127 |
| When Mercy Is Absent | 128 |
| *Autumn Clouds* | 129 |
| The Clearing | 130 |
| Not Only the Extraordinary are Entering the Dream World | 131 |

# I.

# THE JOURNEY

## DAWN

Dawn begins our story in a filter of mist,
new languages in an old land.

We only get a glimpse of life
distant as a bird's trill
lasting as long as a snowflake.

In the absolute quiet,
lost in the curtains of memory,
sunlight deepens a canyon
with purple shadows.

Each day can be like this —
alive, lingering into evening
waiting for a storm
that never accumulates.

## THE ORGAN MOUNTAIN RANGE

1.

At an elevation of about nine thousand feet,
the Chihuahuan Desert bares its teeth-shaped rocks
like an old prospector looking for gold
among the narrow canyons —
all he finds is ponderosa pine.


2.

The Potrillo Mountains are the furthermost
location of the mind, inaccessible
as memory. Thirst does not make distance
closer, nor knowing that to the northeast
is a convenience store in Las Cruces.
It has the most inconvenient hours
and is always sold out of water, beer, and Coke.
Cinder cones lay all over the place.


3.

Sometimes anger flows
like these prehistoric lava flows did.
The place in your brain overheats
and creates these craters,
giant thumbprints in the land.

4.

In the jagged canyons of twisted emptiness,
Billy the Kid rode hard-fast trying to lose
the posse he long lost.
Looking over his shoulder,
he saw the distance between yesterday
and today, trailing behind.
If he rode fast enough,
he could outrun Death and Taxes.


5.

Arroyos is a fancy name for these abysses.
I have left the Chihuahuan desert grasslands
of the Sierra de las Uvas Mountains,
and now I am dizzy, disoriented,
on a peak above Broad Canyon.

I reflect on how hollow my life is.
A shadow crosses over my head,
a cloud vanishing
before it can think of rain.

6.

In the Robledo Mountains,
pre-dinosaur footprints are left behind
to frustrate creationists —
a memo to existence: *I was here.*

In these twisting canyons
of the Broad Canyon Country,
there are petroglyphs on the walls
from three separate Native American cultures.
One is a picture of a fish
surrounded by dancing swirl of dots
like a van Gogh starry night,
and of all things,
a painting of human footprints.
Where were these footprints running from?


7.

Across the grasslands,
I find the Butterfield Stage route
stitching through
hundreds of thousands of acres
of remote hunting.

Organ Mountain pincushion cactus
with its orange flowers
means I just missed a rainfall
by a day or two.

Missed opportunities are like that —
if you are too busy being contemplative,
you just might miss what is front of you.

## AT MOUNTAIN CREST

At the blank-faced cliff edge's
easternmost peak, in the last
choking sunlight,

the heart knows quickness.
The wind is directionless
from this unspoiled earth.

Before the moment is erased,
this entire world throbs, pulses away —
even the breakneck river tries to get away.

\*

There is an insurrection of light over color and air.
There are no stragglers of clouds.
Weather is approaching beastly over rocks.

A spray of birds is squawking into the bright light
and disappearing
as if into a hole into another earth.

There is a weakness in the distant horizon.
There seems to be fire coming off this certainty.
The river does not stay around long enough to find out.

\*

There is a dizzy tightness of the heart
while sitting on this sideways tilting rock face.
The rock could go any moment, take me with it

into the nothingness,
with its rushing flow-sound rapids,
like birds flushing aimlessly or startled breath.

The river takes my thoughts far away
to empty. I cannot see where
they break into stepped-on twigs.

## TEENAGERS HIKING IN THE FOREST

*a pantoum*

A rampant creek breaking the fabric of earth
below blossoms feverously making fruit,
my heart leapt like trout as she opened her bra.
I had my hands full of eager, hot intent,

below, blossoms feverously making fruit.
It began to drizzle. Smelling of pheromones,
I had my hands full of eager, hot intent.
Like goldenrod, I was spreading my seed in air.

It began to drizzle smelling of pheromones.
We were on black bottom land, deep center,
like goldenrod. I was spreading my seed in air.
The sky was blue like admiring eyes.

We were on black bottom land. Deep center
was always unrequited love, always echoing.
The sky was blue like admiring eyes,
or evening primroses, or blue jays in hawthorns

always unrequited love. Always echoing;
always disappearing — love was fickle,
or evening primroses, or blue jays in hawthorns —
love was wildness, flight and settling in,

always disappearing. Love was fickle;
a rampant creek was breaking the fabric of earth.
Love was wildness flight and settling in.
My heart leapt like trout as she opened her bra.

## EXPLORING THE MOUNTAIN RANGE

    1.

Writing in a notebook between the arch
of night and yellowing morning,
the mass of unreal mountains
are hazed, wavering with clouds
on their shoulders, white-grey as my hair.

The cloud-movement vacillates, dazed,
whispers footsteps.

    2.

A fresh spring stream, some patches of snow
skipped by sun in the hollowed-out places
behind rock-shade —

some say, these heights are familiar; some say,
they are moonlight illusions,
an invisible compass into a lover's arms,
being welcomed, clouds of wildflowers raining.

3.

After I removed cold touch of snow,
the purple crocus is a bruised heart.

I have arrived at this point
through meadows of light,
found this untouched place,
this geography of love,
opening snow to see tuffs of grass,
flowering grape-colored bulbs
waiting desperately to be found.
The mountain spoke to me
with my wife's voice.


4.

All secrets are not apparitions,
although distance distorts height.

Mountains are never the same as relief maps.
Their flanks are straight-up discovery.
When ascending, it seems lonelier going up.

5.

I have been where the snow remains all year.
I have been close enough to an eagle's nest
to count the eggs and be driven off by diving talons.
I have had my feet fighting with a rock slide.

Now, my mountain climbing days are over,

but not my intense urge
to know every inch of my wife's love.

## CAMPING

    1.

The moon rustled, caught in deer antlers.
An ember in a smothered campfire
snap-cracked its last breath.
A cattail shook in slow wind
on the edge of water and darkness.

I woke, partially afraid, not knowing
where I was, or why the pitch of dark
was blacker than a bear, or why the movement
of stars was hunched over the charcoal clouds.

Now I was more awake than I ever was.
My gasp took me to a place
I had not been since I was a child
checking under a bed for monsters.

    2.

Question marks floated out of the river
like ghosts of stars and curses,
noises we may never hear.

The world closed like a tent.
The sum total of my life, this infinity
beyond stars where frightened lives
and smallness exist, overtook me.

There was no fear that was not my own.

3.

The river was twist-turning over rocks.
There was no shelter under the trees
from noise and memory.


4.

The heart is always restlessly disturbed.

When we are in the landscape of dreams,
that quiet presence, we respond to the world
and all its fleeting assurances.

We are strangers even to ourselves;
we could burn and turn cold as coal;
we could go into storm-fields
trying to brush away low-hanging branches
like a person fighting sleep; and still
we could be seething in silence
as snow reminds us firmly
it is time to hibernate.


5.

To the west, there is a mountain
I know by touch.

The sky is greying.
A freeze is coming arriving late.

Storms chase all memories into the ritual of recovery.

## SNAKE RIVER

    1.

This corkscrew river flows
anywhere except east.
Nothing is quiet:

sound of rapids
appear where there is none,
deathly silent where there is,

never knowing what is ahead,
disappearing,
sometimes white as your knuckles;

sound annihilates other noises —
sounds you have never heard before,
water spouts upwards,

rocks the size of houses,
rocks the size of triceratops,
rocks split open and forced back together.

Water changes directions,
water rushing into itself,
water trying to escape water.

I can only do so much paddling,
when paddling becomes futile
as a black hole appears in mid-stream.

Water appears to be boiling,
cooking up some mischief,
wanting to swallow raft and all.

Three standing 10-foot waves —
"hydraulics"; backwards waterfalls —
all I can do is lash myself in.

It is like falling in love
when everything is out of control,
bailing out makes it worse.

The water ahead drops out of sight.
I know that this cannot be good.
I paddle backwards while pulled forward.

My stomach coils into the river,
side-slipping like a toboggan,
the sides of hills racing the opposite way.

The raft grinds on basalt boulders,
snagging, releasing,
flounders out of water, then nose dives.

I am drenched, air dried, rinsed again,
a bobbin in water,
a free-for-all, oars flapping upon water.

God cannot hear prayers in the roar,
the raft climbing stairs of waves, then —
nothing — the water has left me in air.

2.

This area defies logic.
It meanders
not going anywhere and going fast,

icy lakes, black lava flows,
sagebrush deserts far as the eye sees,
bubbling mud baths, hundreds of ponderosa pines,

a land as lean as hunger,
where if you get lost you stay lost,
a place where you had better come prepared.

It looks like the end of the world.
If water could tear us apart, it would.
If we could stitch ourselves up, we do it again.

The water does not know the difference.
It is never the same twice.
It never makes up its mind long enough.

You will begin to think you will not survive.
The water draws you into its indecision.
It is useless to beg when you are out of control.

Alpine firs entrench their long roots
up glaciers into the thinness soil
like a climber driving a spike and fastening.

During ascent, the air impossible to breathe,
I found a Fool's Huckleberry holding moisture
in dry winds among sedges that have died down

to subterranean stem-tips
as if going into a deep hibernation.
I found a red-leafed wild rose entangled,

embraced by bracken ferns
turned brassy yellow
and copper orange in spare soil,

watered by snow melt-off
down steep talus slopes
of loose rocks and gravel.

It was too soon and doomed.
In the dry mountain air, trees rot slowly,
leaves brown for decades,

shrubs hide behind rocks as if afraid,
among a green wave of young firs.
Trees try to cross the continent,

following streams,
bringing their own rapids.
I can smell smoke before there is fire:

it hangs in swelling clouds;
the air swims with ladybugs.
The wind changes directions like a river.

3.

Eating chokeberries
in the outcropping
pine-dark ridges,

knowing I'd make it —
rough
broken calluses,

scrub trees
impossible to cross,
sun blackened,

desperately searching soil
in the prehistoric lava runs,
yawning holes

the size of Civil War mortars;
there are some things in the world
so willing to survive, they just do.

This is the lament of the land.
A thumb-sized hummingbird with invisible wings
is a faintly audible hum.

This is when all moments break down into clarity,
when things so small can easily startle you with strangeness,
when the sun is lower than the land.

It becomes the resting place for coyote songs.
Ice forms in the caverns of my nostrils,
unwilling to be evicted,

when dampness sets in.
Cutthroat trout in black water
float over my head.

The raft slews around,
sideswiping rocks
in water smelling of sulfur.

It feels endless, hopeless,
and over too quick
like waiting for the first date.

When a mountain climber says
it was interesting, they meant
it damn well near almost killed them.

But when you rock-climb
you get a real feel
what a rock feels.

In the alpenglow — that strange time
in high peaks of first and last light
when it is a blink in between —

rocks glow from within.
You know you've reached a point
where you'll never be again.

The river —
there is no escaping it —
it is everywhere it wants to be.

## FROM THE CLOSENESS OF OAK, WHERE DARK HOLDS BREATH

Bottomland forests at the low end,
drenched by breathless rise,
hard wood saturated,

absorb what is given, and taken.
Hidden small life finds sanctuary
for the temporary.

Survival depends on adaptability —
the ecosystem supports or
it fails, each finding a connection.

Insects carry seeds under a thicket of leaves.
Some accidental planting happens.
Hundreds of butterflies burst out into light —

surprising noise! Silence had been accumulating
like blue herons becoming cumulous,
breathless as the land finding bottom.

## HEAT INDEX BREAKS THE TEMPERATURE GAUGE

it has been a month of high humidity
monotony unbroken

cicadas are indifferent to the heat
opening their satchels of hectoring noises

across the haze is an endless dead mass
of former green pines

droplets of moisture are impatient
hanging in the air like mica

an inadequate breeze
makes for poor laundry

birds are afraid their wings would melt
cats are too scorched to think straight

## DRY SPELL

it has been a long dry spell

we need an inundation
large wheelbarrows of drenching rain
rain beating its knuckles on the roofs
like woodpeckers searching diseased trees for insects

drops might sizzle

we need a thrashing rain
cloud-smashing

rain so fierce
salmon mistake it for upstream
begin spawning
all the way into the sky

it has been so long since it has rained
cattle smash the wire fence
to reach an imaginary river

## THIRD WARNING

The maple trees smelled the burning metals
from the chemical plant
and cried in the dwindling sundown,
sending out extra maple wings to ensure their future,
knowing how rough times were arriving,
and people were hiding their responsibilities.

I left in morning scarlet light, leaves trembling,
my lips delivering hard, uncomfortable news.
The warning was everywhere —
like pulverized seashells.

## IT IS DRIZZLING HEAT

It was ninety degrees with humidity topping a hundred,
and the heat felt atrocious
until reading it was one hundred and twenty-two in India
where the roads had melted.

Here the haze was merely white blossoms of agony,
and the residue of moisture disappears before forming.
In India, their minds must have been cooking
with their eyes feeling like fried eggs.

Some politician denies climate change,
and car tires in India explode.
Somewhere, night promises more heat for tomorrow.
Politicians must have air conditioner hearts.

The angry god of furnaces depletes water to bone.
Somewhere, a rich person wonders about the fuss.
I have it good, comparatively speaking, to India.
Politicians have assured me heat is in my imagination.

## **EXTREME HEAT**

Light penetrates trees into yellow dust,
splitting elements of wind and air.
In this fiery heat, grass becomes raw purple.

This light has a way of contorting trees,
like forging metal. Hot breath.
Whispers inside the light say the storms have left.

The yellow inside the midpoint is white emptiness
where noise is liquefied. It blinds anyone
into deafness. The woods begin moldering.

If you rub a hand across a glass of water,
it vibrates like a tuning fork.
Tones have a way of raising and lowering in pitch.

Like unsettled air and light, in this high frequency,
you never would notice the adjustment:
an owl's wing readying for shifting flight winds.

## **RAIN PATTERNS**

The mysterious eyes of rain had concentrated,
purple and distant in the high branches like plums.

Not one drop, but a multitude. Not a grace note,
but a symphony where none of the musicians
have the same sheet music. Not an ending
spread out like a tablecloth,
but the disappointment of a supper
cold and forgotten when someone is late.

But it rained, nonetheless,
a temperamental child kicking and screaming.

## INEXPLICABLE RAIN

1.

In black raspberry darkness,
we are all the same music,
notes raining fast and slow,

crossing long fields of uncut wheat,
just before harvest,
wheat tips brushing calloused hands.


2.

Inexplicable rain brings conversations:
battens-down fields, a storm of prayers,
someone knocking on a door.


3.

Lightning crackled a bad radio connection,
boundary line bushes heavy with rain,
tilt the driveway.

3. Suite in G major

We ruin the waters at our own peril.
This is dissonant music, tainted, polluted
sounds, smashing atoms. Not one living object
could survive the lack of water, not one
could drink with sewage and survive,
although cruel politicians say otherwise
while refusing to taste-test what is offered.

Someday, when the water is rust colored,
will generations exclaim,
*What were they thinking?* Will survivors adapt?
I know I won't be here to witness it.

All I can do is dip my hands
into cautionary words,
raise them up, beg for forgiveness,
let it wash over us
with soothing rain, hope
forgiveness is enough, hope it drenches,
pray water returns life to the earth.

Let the music of purifying rain fall
where rain will to do the most good,
the swelling of an orchestra
before the big climax.

## THE DAY THEY STOLE THE WATER

The transparency was a smooth, slow, clear river
staying barely long enough to be there
to hold a decent conversation, yet very patient,
providing time to stall some people
to be soothed by light undulating on its surface.
You could hear this river as it slid by
taking the soft plop of a turtle.

I left that peace hijacked by a war I did not believe in,
for a country that could not care less
if I dipped my toes in holy water
or tasted from the same stream tadpoles began.

When I returned, for it is possible to survive
war and drowning and insane political policies,
the river had been forcibly removed.

Progress had drained it, planting suburban homes
full of blinking distant messages
of television fulfillment, if only
we bought stuff we never needed.

So, I lost that river.

There is no map of it or the past,
and the area had become a modified place
no good for a self-respecting frog or person.

## WIND SHEAR

The precision of grief-rain brings
persistent silence,
flecks of lyrically simple drops
changing warm ground to cold,
making cirrus clouds low to the ground.

Fog lofts, like a great blue heron,
looping and shredding outwards
into the ruddy daybreak. Rain ponders
over the land, rifting blues call
and response from a down-on-her-luck
woman who has been-done-seen-it-all,
been there and back more times
then she cares to count.

But then, sonorous lilting arias
cheer onward. Remnants of music forge
all the way to the mountain laurel.

## SURVIVAL DEPENDS UPON YOUR DEFINITION OF RECOVERY

The national weather service declared this hurricane season.
The news was late.
We were already picking up between storms.

The wind wound up again,
ready to throw another curve ball.
A black helicopter hovered above like a giant mosquito.

According to a national reporter,
this hurricane was not a major one.
But to us, a tree crashing through a roof was significant.

## THERE IS DARKNESS TO THE WATER

*a villanelle*

There is darkness to water
of intent and revenge for what we've done,
as the earth becomes hotter and hotter.

What will we tell our sons and daughters?
In our destruction, what have we won?
There is darkness to the water.

It thirsts for revenge and in its anger
it flattens cities, ending what we begun,
causing the earth to become hotter and hotter.

Who were the leaders? Why did they falter?
Our forests, ruined land, both made barren.
There is darkness in the water.

What will we tell children after?
We ruined the earth and all we were given,
and made the air sulfur, becoming hotter.

Now we cannot go back. The winds stir
nothing and we cannot alter
the intense darkness in the water
which floods as things get hotter.

## ROWING

The boat dock settled and tilted into brackens.
Silver fish heads were cut for gull feed.
The dock was rotted, and tossed fish heads glanced
off, glassy-eyed, towards rippling light
on black-ebbing waves.

I rowed towards the epicenter of the lake,
far from the cove or recognizable coastline
until I could not see the sloops and topmasts.

I could take as long as it takes to get there.
There was no rush. I heard the oars rubbing
against oarlocks, prompting forward
towards that clear place where fish circled.
The pull of lure and bobbins was strong.
I went beyond the dark splashes of pines.

In loneliness, distance pushed the hull
wanting to return before sun-drop
to the cottages with hung fishing nets
before a nor'easter tore at my face.
The water was luminous slivers
like cigarette smoke of cursive writing
insisting I stay.

Somewhere, back in the unknown distance,
stricken houses of palsied framework waited
for any kind of news.

## MARCH

It's rain-making.
Something permanent in the stone steps
is repelling rain. It stops me short,
makes me draw in my breath,
count my blessings.

It is cold, this steady rain.
But, in your heart, there, it is bristling with love.
You are writing words from March rain.
It is enough to bruise the stone of any heart.
This kind of drenching can fly into the landscape of your bones.

## RELEASING THE DARK LANDSCAPE

Last sunlight falls behind the vanishing trees,
where it hesitates before leaving completely.
Some decisions are measured by regret.
Some of us, when we find ourselves old, notice this.

Out on the prairie, someone tries to hold the land
together with barbed wire stapled to aging wood posts.
However, I am the kind of person who brings cutters
and snips each sharp wire, letting the fields open.

I am the kind who encourages yellow-throated meadowlarks.
When cut, the dark will be released; the air will be set free.
Doors on distant houses will ripple like muscles after working.
Some wonder why I do this, question idleness as the cause,

suggest I had nothing better to do. Laws are made
to discourage people like me from acting impulsively.
I cannot obey, and I sharpen blades into a raptor's talons.
I am the kind that knows outcrops sweeten with silence.

I go to the wire to test it. It glints in moonlight and speaks.
It knows the quiet patterns of flight, the tactical for listening.
I should have brought the cutter, its slender purpose of justice.
The rusting wind caught on it should be freed. I touch
    barehanded.

It slices like eyes. It whispers, *Be careful.* The fields say, *Spare me.*
Yearning and ceasing are shadows lengthening, in stillness,
in the final ambient light; then, the meadowlark stopped —
only the robin's sleepy-time sound is in this field, and it is held there.

I experience the necessary absence. I also lose blood to its danger.
They say actions speak for you and what you stand for.
I have been listening to the suffering. Something had to be done.
When I cut, the earth flies away — wings or leaves or regret.

## CLEAR-CUT

The trees are clear-cut, burnt brush
baring the skull of the mountain
when emptiness slopes
a highway
to the vanishing point of land and sky.

And if we drift upwards
through stumps, pitched pines, dogwood,
jackdaws, leveled purple loosestrife,
all cleared and hacked away now
for some forgotten reason,
we will get close to what makes no sense —

our ambitions are empty black bags.

## THE GLASS-FACED DEER OF BOONVILLE, NEW YORK

After they roped it while riding snowmobiles,
they branded it with death camp numbers.
It was caged for a Christmas display.
The deer rattled antlers on the breakproof glass
and children asked if it could fly.

One night, someone let it loose
and it broke into a grocery store,
eating carrots and wild blueberries.
Then, it ran as the moon runs
behind clouds and migrating geese,
never caught by a pack of snowmobiles.

## THE LILAC BUSHES AND THE FOREST-TENT CATERPILLARS

Lilacs grew on our boundary.
My window opened to a whiffed aroma of lilacs.
Light-purple light would wake me.

There was a thin spider-web nest of caterpillars.
In the weight of their nest squirmed black larvae,
begging for mercy. The larvae moved together single file.
Silken treads were laid down by leaders.
They knew they were going places
and they were destroying things in the way.
Buff-colored moths emerged about 10 days later.
They searched the solitude of streetlights.
The neighbors tried smoking the nest to kill it.

This is how I learned that some things must die.
This was the lie of peaceful co-existence.
The nest would return;
smoke would return, the lilacs would return,
the neighbors would try eradication.

I could hear the caterpillars dying.

Everything is a by-product of disagreement.
Everything that was is gone.
Everything that will be is not possible anymore.

And in the end, nothing survived.
The neighbors passed on.
My father turned purple as a lilac, and died.
There are no more moths hovering on streetlights.
There are no lilac neighborhoods.

There is nothing left to argue about.
Some army follows a blue line over boundaries.
Some moon is disjointed in the darkness of larvae.

## SILK WORMS

They whisper in trees.

We never did know how to do things quietly.
The noise of our factories ate forests, devoured rivers.
This is a part of us.
We ignore small voices.
Some things die so other things survive.
The forests are cleared emphatic statements to this belief.

We are so enormous
we cannot see nests of silk moths hanging like Japanese lanterns.

We killed them off.
Then the trees vanished:
the Silver Maple; Hickory; Walnut — gone.
With the trees went our textile plants and jobs.

When we are finally alone, nothing speaking to us,
Will we finally understand the fabric of things?
How everything is spun thinly and fragile.

Will we will hear whispering
inside our body, where it had been all along?

## THE WIRE FENCE HOLDING BACK THE WORLD

*"I place my feet/with care in such a world"*
— The Well Rising, *by William Stafford*

Light ripples at sunrise
against large dark chunks of breaking night,
and the moon folds behind blistered skies
lit by coal-ember light.

Light is wavering,
asking to withdraw from hovering this world.
Light drinks from sharp rocks
in purple shadows. Birds crash through sunbreak.

What have I achieved matching this?
I hear pleading long after bird-flight
curled over the hills, measuring all
who do not listen.

*

Here is where I dig in —
spade breaking soil in intermittent rain
and sun, between gasp and fear,
before this world goes all the way to forgetfulness.

Before harvest and seed fail,
I want this house where trails begin and end,
where light is crystals
and promises are rewarded. Here light comes —

down the hills, touching every leaf,
making them hum. My face feels sun
as the ground deepens brown, finding tree stumps
and voles slinking in wet, uncut grass.

I grip hard on this world. I won't let go —
although a faraway voice calls to me,
I make the hard decision to stay. Here,
light shocks. I cut a barbed wire fence.

## WHAT I WANT

I want the kind of morning that lasts
well beyond the everlasting glimmers
and brushes against your body like strung beads
used as a curtain to the entrance to your heart.
These beads should clatter
sounding ever so very much like sleet on hard surfaces.

I want the kind of preserved peace my father felt
after working so hard, seemingly getting nowhere,
as he went deep into the cave of silence
like a hermit crab goes into a larger shell.
His inward spiral would find the edges
towards a center, where nothing could disturb,
a quiet that contemplates. This peace
would fill the stretched-out face of the morning.

I want the diamond-faceted eyes of a bee
seeing everything all at once, everywhere.
I do not want to miss seeing anything.
Those eyes would not blink or flinch
from horror, but would see it for itself —
the disturbance of peace, the rendering of it,
the mute silence afterwards
when everyone realizes how bad it was.

This peace would be a different peace —
more of shock and shame. We would wonder
if reconciliation was possible,
hoping we drained ourselves enough
to be sensible about peace.

I want my eyes to see the changing heart
in the sun as it knows peace and silence.

What I want is not unreasonable.
What I want is not impractical.
What I want is not unattainable.
What I want is what all people want:

the silence that is common and essential;
the silence that flourishes;
the silence that rolls loose as a pebble
under the feet of someone climbing towards peace.

I want the silence that will become surrogate stories
we can tell generations, proud of our accomplishments,
stories filling a basket with sunbeams.

Sometimes, things just open up,
like the sun emerging from a conch shell,
or a mountain growing out of our palms
because our breath is the stillness of cranes.
When we speak, bees sting the wicked
with forgiveness, or beads like a rosary
click on our eyes silently when we search
for the peace our fathers never found
while grinding their teeth at the moon.

You asked me what I would want
for my grandchildren. What came to me
was thunder and the silence between
when lightning strikes. How you can count it
to figure out how close it is. How the flash
lasts inside your eyes, even when you close them.

How when lightning stitches across the sky
to ground, it is like an old treadle sewing machine
that does not have a back-stitch. How the rain
has different ways of falling and different sounds,
and how it dictates the length of the rainfall.

How my father would walk in rain to feel it
against his face like sandpaper
to know what God wanted from him.
How his pacing was slow regardless of the rain,
like the rain could not salve whatever was within him.
How the silence was not enough. How drenched
his eyes flash-flooded
until he could barely see where he was going
and could care less when he would come back.
How the bees never stung him.
How stitched we are together.
How nothing is the same when we find the sublime.

## LOSS

A wailing loss from the branches crosses valleys
to distant villages. People are too busy,
and do not hear the anguish.
No one hears the keening wind.
Where does this wind and lack of listening end?
Certainly not at the unlatched garden gate.

## *ABOVE THE SPRING TÂF*

*Painting by Guy Manning*

The steep hill towards the sun through the white pine
is where woodpeckers knock searching for insects.
In this spring where you can still feel young,

there is a different kind of silence when sounds
are more intense, where you can hear grass in wind,
singing about the on-coming light rain
where light itself rains between the drops
tapping on pine needles like tuning forks.

All the absence in your life is filled. There is no need to rush
through damp grass towards sunlight. It will be there
when you need it. Just listen to the katydid
and spring water after ice melt clears its throat.
Above the spring leaves, the stars are greening.
If we climb these hills, we might reach them before we die.

## FOREST

    1.

At the edge of every forest is
a demarcation line, a flame
of breathlessness.

We either enter
as if opening the forest's chest cavity
to find its heart
needing surgery, or
we dissolve
into bitter leaves,
throwing ourselves into that breathlessness,
never seeing what is exposed
for transient vision,
or we linger too long
doubting
what disturbance we bring.


    2.

What is entered
is left behind,
a rubble of what used to be.

Even these words trail behind
in dangling breeze.

## IN THE HIGH HILLS

In the high hills, trees shake their fists
to the surprise of sky.

Blackbirds are blown through sky
into the other world
where things are never empty,
filling the landscape —
*more* —
into necessary readings.

In this other world,
distance is unknown —
no one has a word for it.

I want to go there soon,
soon as I am taken.

## **BELOW THE BEECH, ABOVE THE TÂF**

*Painting by Guy Manning*

I would lie on my back, looking into leaves
until the world was out of focus,
pointless dots for impressionistic painters.

What I was doing was seeing beyond
what we were meant to see and seeing it.

As the trees became blurred lines
I could see right through them.
The world beyond was no longer invisible
or strange, or faraway, or impossible to get to.

The real world, the one we are not meant to see,
has been hidden and hard to imagine.

I return there, whenever I can.
Age never stopped me; I always Believe.
A part of me is already in that ghostly Other World.

## MORNING

The first light against the breaking sky
humming with disturbed insects.

Love can be everywhere and nowhere,
where mistakes are not blameless,
not disappearing around the bend of light.

Even the rushes at the edge of a lake
know to rush towards light.

When darkness comes, and it will,
every part will feel sorrow
descending its long ladder.

## SPRING

Through the doorway of spring's dawn
the voice of a slow river shushes
to get somewhere over rocks.

Our released breath scatters wood ducks
creating noise and disturbed rustling air.

A tree is twisted like a man turning
three-quarters to see what is behind him
and not expecting what he found.

The river finds its way to the tree.
What one says to the other is unclear.

There are whispers of light in the leaves.

Grief shadows everything in our path.
Water embroiders us to land, tree, and sky.
Milkweed's pink flowers are drops of silence.

The river rubs against rock, making mud clouds,
reminding us the world is an unsettled place.

No one can find what is not searched for.
Change is a risk some find unacceptable.

What is not acceptable is the unwillingness to try.

## DEFEATED

He tried to fight the wind blowing him back.
He had an urgency to get somewhere
and lost, cursing like an artesian,
the language of failure.
Every wish he'd ever had was taken,
torn down, blasted, shot-gunned —
every brilliant idea, tossed into a ravine.

He could take a survey of his life and find
nothing but debris, the knife edges of insults,
to degrees of separation, the longing
always returning like a plague.

Every failure was razor-sharp —
the steel mill closed, windows rock-smashed
and turning blind eyes; the stillborn
he had no money to bury properly;
the calico blotches found in his chest x-ray.

He couldn't keep this up.
He'd done this for far too long.

When he went into the bar, he wanted to fight,
be stomped on, bleed out, and maybe,
just maybe, then, the pain would end.

There was so much sadness wherever he looked.

## SPEAKING THE LANGUAGE OF DEER

She heard a thumping sound behind her house,
turned on the back-porch light to
a small herd of deer
startled by the suddenness of light, frozen
and indecisive as a letter of regret.

"Don't worry; it's just me. I won't harm you,"
she coaxed, a voice in light snowfall.

The deer transfixed,
disbelieving in all things human
and unnatural,

the darkness between them, a division,
an unsettling
beyond light and resolution,
assessing danger on the fly,

hindquarters enveloping into darkness
as slow as words
determined as if by a Quaker weighing options
*within the Light*, in silence.

The woman in the household wondered
where the deer came from, which imaginary forest,
how the deer survived in the city
without encountering a car, how hooves
might feel on concrete after being in the meadows,

why dark was a prevailing wind,
how their eyes remained after the deer were gone,
how her purse was genuine deerskin,
how it fit everything in neat compartments
like she fit in her apartment,

how she could still hear their refusal to stay.

## LOST

Geese get lost in mist, sidetracked
in heavy stillness, dew-wings
from burn-off, just around the corner
of mountains no one can see
but remember are there, reliable
as geese calling out to each other.

Some are unable to follow the lead,
break from the pattern. Their sounds
bounce off clouds and mountains.
Stillness is stirred from the low ground,
biting the air. At noon, still, no one can see.

It might get worse. It is better to sit tight,
hope for the weather to shift, clouds lifting
like a flock of geese over transparent lakes.

## II.

## LOVE IS A JOURNEY

## HOW TO FIND LOVE

The metallic-blue damselfly
unfolds its wings.
Above is a squabble of geese.

We should be asking:
is it enough to untether my heart?

Daylight is crumbling. Everywhere is insisting:
Look!
Look at me! Look at me!

Whatever we are doing, it is never enough.

There are stories we tell ourselves,
embellishing them over time —
water moving silt, changing patterns.
We want to be where we never belong.

Say what you want about the blue damselfly
and its short life of flutter and jerk;
it knows where it's going, where it belongs,
where it desires to be.
It never settles for second-best;
it is always searching,
always wanting to see more.

Say what you want
about the clap of geese flooding into light;
this is an entirely normal day,
churning clouds like backwash, riptide,
brimming with stars or no words.

I know where the strained light goes
when it's dragged behind the earth's curve.

What can we say after that?

## SOME THINGS YOU CAN NEVER REPAIR

We were repairing the sagging porch.
"It's dangerous to fall in love," says the man,
"it means you will fall hard."
We had ripped off all the warped boards,
installing a fifteen-degree incline.

There were yellow poppies as far as we could see.
Evening would be coming home soon.
After a while we would not be able to see to nail.
There was the smell of wet peat moss
ripening like a hand releasing secrets.

His wife was finally resting, her body curled
like a tulip bulb. The stars went out
like birthday candles. One last streak of purple
dwindled like being raked.

We talked about the close baseball game,
the cost of vegetables today, oldies music.
Our words and hands refused to quit.
Neither of us could talk about the obvious —
his wife was shrinking into herself until she died.

## I CANNOT STOP PAIN

Canada geese are leaving everyone behind
without a hint of what to do next.
We are clueless, emptying like branches.

Our future is in the clouds, in the entrails
of the gut-shot deer pulling itself through
the woods to hide.

There is a way to get lost in all of this.
Geese keep trying to exit, flying blindly into head-
winds, into the fading yellow, into the bloody sunset.

## WHY DARKNESS WHIMPERS

A longing becomes impossibly larger,
gnawing at the underbrush
like a person biting off syllables
when telling us less than necessary.

Darkness only wanted to find its way home,
but blindness made it tap here
and here, smelling for the familiar,
sounds echoing off what was missing.

It is the way absence converges with remoteness,
strained in its sense of direction,
and darkness missed what it did not have anymore.
This story does not end well.

Wherever darkness went, it never knew where to stay.
How many of us experience this loss at least once?
Whatever vanishes is not always permanently gone
as long as we hope for regaining what is missing.

## VAN GOGH'S *STARRY NIGHT*

When darkness-filled madness
shudders trees, spreading into each leaf,
it's a wonder if any of us would be left
standing as a barometer of stillness —

not shaken, not lost. Whatever radiance
we have had would leave us, we'd feel
abandoned, lost in an impression of voices
no one ever hears.

Surely, our bones would turn blue
from this churning. The sun
would clamp down on the remaining music
trying desperately to release such anguish.

## FIRST SPRING MORNING

Spring has an obsession: say everything all at once
before it all fades away into the unremarkable.
The light in the backyard releases a thrush's shadow.

I am astonished into an overwhelming silence,
grinded into silt. I have been given
and entrusted with this sliver of forever.

I know what I have to do: witness
all the ingredients trying to blend together
and report what I've seen.

With such immense facts coming my way,
I can't catch them all. But I try.
I have such unquenchable thirst.

## LISTENING INTO THE SILENCE

In the quiet, morning is unburdened —
the sky a hibiscus color:
curious love.

Day begins.
Abundance cascades of birdsong —
omens just a heartbeat away,

elegies of living
when we feel too much,
poised to learn what we need to know —

this inescapable realization
of entering into the marvelous!

Too soon, the moment is over.
Light understands
the unexpected, the lament,
the surrender, the cold unsettling
surprising force of wonder and loss.

I listen into the silence
for instructions, hoping
a voice will answer,
not from within,
but from *otherworldliness*.

**TWENTY REASONS**

I can name more than twenty reasons to love you,
but I was too busy thinking about what to say,
when you snuck up behind me,
hugged me like I might turn to air,
and you didn't want to let go
and neither did I.

## THE GIFTS

Darkening, rapid heartbeats
invite me to a home
waiting to dream. In night's ocean,
sea anemone stars
hold shimmering scraps of light.

I share these with you — blossoms
of endless love, batting
for a quilt, as I spill seeds of light,
constellations always expanding
from whirls on our fingertips, movement
of ecstatic starlings.

This is what I bring to you —

bundles to sway you
and haze from shadow-trees
turning the fretboard of your heart,
making our music in tune.

## SIX LOVE POEMS

    1.

I say your name —
a butterfly in a windless day
dissolves into windchimes.

I repeat your name —
twice, ample rain arrives
stone-deaf to my pleas.

Three times, I call —
no one is there,
moving to where I can't see
into this world
still writing itself.


    2.

No day is like today.
Stillness is bound to land,
a holiness I've forgotten.

Love travels the lifeline
in your palm, interrupted
by intersections.

Love explores longing:
restless as fireflies
disturbed by absence.

There is no day
exactly like today;
you are not here.


3.

Love is not senseless
since I've found you.

I want to be around you,
swirls of calm rain.

A breath
rising from water,

Sound
finding its way to be heard.

A mesmerizing dance
requiring two people.


4.

Like false eyes on a butterfly,
I can't see if you're here.

My heart dances over milkweed,
searching for you.

5.

I can't find you.
Someone moved the world.

What I thought were your tracks
going into accumulating snow,
vanishing ahead, belonged to a train.
Parts of the tracks were removed.
The important parts.
The metal ties,
the hammered spikes,
the wooden cross beams
holding it all together
like wishes for things to be different.

They were taken away.
Now, I can't find you.

I can't follow you
into that *other* world.


6.

I can't find you.
Your past was removed.

That's why I reached
the end of the line.

That's why I still have
a ticket in my hand.

## DAY LILIES

The roots of the day lilies take over like armies,
interlocking and twisting over
and under each other like French braids,
making it impossible to uproot
or transplant, often appearing elsewhere,
determined as a teenager to get their way —

then explosions of color open dramatically
making me regret yanking them out —

in my dreams they overwhelm the earth,
lifting my house off its foundation,
its roots are tentacles encasing me —

I am tangled in the sheets,
window open, letting in day-lily light.

## AN EXALTATION OF LARKS

*term for a gathering of larks; also their collective sounds*

The ground is creeping with them in a field of short plants,
matching the bare earth, stirring the world
through high tinkling music. More aggregations
numbering in the hundreds swirl in winter skies
their songs. They are praising the air, the land, even
the dry, dead grass nesting between snow melt.
They exalt intensely. They are jazz notes from Miles Davis
punctuating what is felt, birthing the cool, the extravagant.

We should be so draped in joy, with such be-bop happiness.
Larks understand it is better to congregate to celebrate,
let loose blasts of flare and tribute — all collaboration,
raw interpretation, innovation — snowflakes of music notes;
acclaiming and proclaiming without restraint;
fierce jubilation in the harshest, coldest times.

## THE MOMENT STILLNESS MOVES

My ears shadow the sparrow-sound from branch
to high ash branch, behind leaves where I cannot see it.

A branch twangs as a crow leaves the area
to complain about what he has witnessed.

I am practicing the art of staying still like a kingfisher
edging near enough to strike at images of fish.

I haven't moved, although the sun wallowed
in both the river and wistful sky like a Japanese woodcut.

I wait so long the black flies never notice me.
The sparrow keeps juggling music.

Crow complains he's heard this song thousands of times.
A branch waves for an encore.

The sparrow plunges through the solo like an arrow
to the heart of the matter: there is not enough music.

I still haven't moved an inch, not a twitch,
although the music moves me, rippling water.

## LONGING IS LIKE THE SEED

> *"Longing is like the seed"*
> *— Emily Dickinson, #1255*

Inside our longing is a thirst —
a canticle of Silence, a constant desire to be,
to be sustained in Silence,
to relinquish what holds us back.

Attentiveness is required. To find the tranquil,
one needs to Center in ambience of muted night sky —
to be a small, moving noise, heightening in Silence —
to be in the Presence of things we never heard.

We not need say anything —
yet an overpowering urge compels us to.
The here and now is gone — the endlessness remains.
It is there, in a storm or quiet, before or in the wake after.

## AT THE END OF THE DAY

At the end of the day, Grandfather Moon
is wearing his long johns,
lighting the stars with a single match.
Grandmother Stories picks up her knitting
of bright colors, saving remnants for another day.

## AFTER SERVICE

Autumn leaves congregate in a rain gutter
singing psalms — peace in the valley
contagiously swells out — but a preacher
doubts anyone is listening.

## MIRACLES ARE A DIME A DOZEN

He willed the ocean to approach and willed it back.
The water sighed like a gull's cry.
The sky darkened into slate.
The water lifted and separated into the air.

When the boy's parents had suggested
he should learn self-control,
this was not what they had in mind.

## CLEAR FOR MILES AND MILES

In the flawlessly stilled empty sky
day-stars are noticeable.
A relative smallness presses its thumb hard;
the sky becomes a great heron.
We are caught staring, open-mouthed.
We are cut free, on fire, voicelessly healed.

## HATCHING

A lark jets off into the vague, dry-brush clouds.
Today's news is preempted by this wildness,
this zing.
The cattails are still trying to find the right words
to be able to write up this excitement
directly upon the chicory sky.

Miniature suns, buttercups are
brightening, jolting, transfixing.
Crickets chirr.
Tall, light-tan, feathery weeds signal
their semaphores.

What is that slip of excitement that lark carries?
It threads a needle
into the emptying sky, stitching
love songs into that fabric
so that we are all included, none left behind,
none abandoned or forsaken,
none standing at a fence.

That bird leaves its tarmac,
stirring the world into action,
lifting music as it soars
until its notes stipple
across sheets of water.

Like that lark, we can all transport good news.
No one should squander their opportunity
to enter the chorus of the universe.

# III.

# MEDITATION AS A JOURNEY

## WALKING HILL SLOPES

I walk up hill slopes
of layered pine needles
to hear the snap through fall-dip

to focus on what is essential
what I can forget
the humming winds

twisting branches
like feeling the fibers of a feather
I am home

away from the sour-stench city
I can dream this is reality everywhere
sometimes I do not want to turn back

I want to shed my skin like pine needles
when I get like this
I remember why I come back here

and go back there
how can I appreciate what I have
without knowing the difference

## THE BIRD COUNT

moving in the grey
day among seedless
trees following tracks

blue shadows in snow
by a deserted train station
near a frozen lake

no open water
for kingfishers
we are the only sound

this deserted place
too cold for birds
the clouds never lifted

their grey wings
covered with ice
we cannot see our hands

clustered cardinals
a dense field of red
on the ashen ground

## NIGHTTIME

sitting on a porch swing
watching hush take over
towards the rain-soaked leaves
beyond where the creek is swelling
night-clouds crossing
like buffalo stampeding over hardscrabble fields

I was nearly expecting blind angels
trudging the highway

all these dark silences
we don't know what to do with them
all these ways to turn back
all the ways to know the unseen

## ARGUMENT

the sky is brooding
clouds threaten to never return
as they drove away into the unknown
almost forgetting
what they were waiting for

## SOMEDAY THE WORLD WILL SHUDDER LIKE THIS

in the field of strangeness
there are acres of black leaves
making soft noises as frost

in the scattering
small animals return at dusk
before they can be frozen to death

even now they sense this
approaching like huge thumbs
prying them open

it begins with the speckled leaves
it begins with the years of parting
never ending

daylight already knows too much about dust
someone drags out nets of suspicious water
a quiet is possible but not practical

a distance of birds is not seen
in the absence there is a noise unlike other noises
the sky is a layer of thin skin shaking

it ends with ducks darkening the center of the sky
impetuous singing like static electricity
it ends with someone cursing down a red moon

## ON A RAINY DAY

there are times when morning rains in
the windows beg for more than grey light
we notice
we have lost a day somewhere
yearning does not do any good

it is the same as following a path
narrowing into disappearance
waiting for help in an isolated area will not help
ducks can glide down all they want
but if there is no marsh there is no water
there is no shelter for foolishness

when a sudden storm races faster than sound
all anyone can do is wait it out
all anyone can do is remain calm

sadness works that same slow way

## TANKA

three unripe persimmons are yesterday
not wasting words
with the nothing it has forgotten
telling one secret
generation to generation

## REVITALIZING

what morning has not known the mountain it must cross
its snowcap and melt around a single spring flower

the blue slate sky fills with zeppelins of clouds
every day a new restoration
a new promise
generations never quite the same twice

this is nothing we can hold still

mornings come
regardless of season
politics
or weather's meanness

mornings go
like the passage of laughter or sadness
the sky and land are sewn together
parting like lips
when light is an aura
closing when sighing with nightfall

a story settles down for the night
curls its magnificent differences
trying not to wonder

## WHEN LIGHT REACHES US

in all of eternity not even the stars are forever
when stars die unimaginably distances away
it takes thousands of years for the message
of their passing to reach us

in Amish country the news of death
takes long to reach us by horse and buggy
you hear the horse clip clop on gravel
before the news hitches to a fence post

a man's face has the harshness written on it
you can feel the weight of his responsibility
he had time to compose this bad news
it is clear on his face as pockmarks on a moon

he has time and distance invested in silence
to contemplate an answer that God's intention
for us to die is not arbitrary but it is in fact
written into everywhere if we look and see it

it is in every face every heart every plant
every animal in the land in air even in grief
light reaches us from far or near
from the hard-driven sun or from lamplight

or fireplace or faraway constellations
to every place touched and listening
like a horse listens for commands
the Amish take that weight and recognize it

take that awful responsibility
reflect on it in silence to consider it
like a scientist investigates a star exploding
then all distance is relative when it is death or light

## PACIFIC TREEFROG

the breeding ponds are busy with males
shouting in unison to attract females
the choruses can be startlingly loud
considering the size of this frog

the breeding call is a two-syllable
krek-ek
instead of the one syllable c-r-r-ick
heard the rest of the year
especially during rainstorms

after mating
the females lay small clusters of eggs
attaching them to bits of vegetation
in quiet
shallow water

this is how I should have mated

I could have watched our eggs
as clear drops of pearls
floating near waterlilies

tell me it's not too late
tell me you hear my desperate two-syllable chanting
over all the other males
reaching between the high branches
searching for you
the perfect one
the only one

tell me you will respond
tell me that you are waiting in the quiet
only your green eyes surfaced above pond water
your skin the color of algae

tell me you will croak my name during and after
tell me you will sing your joy loudly
and disturb the smooth sheen of the pond
tell me you will want to hold me closer
the only voice out of many singers
tell me we will have many changelings
tell me the pond will sing of our love

if you tell me these whispers
I will climb the trees right into the sky
right into that green pond above us
right to the clustered eggs of stars
and there I will sing loudest of all
there I will sing new suns and infinite swellings

and it will all be for you
and you will sing back only to me
and it will be our song and only our song
and our children will sing it
the woods will sing it
this singing will be a vast pond
it will be a mild spring shower
a drop at a time
a metronome
a calm heartbeat afterwards

this is what I would sing
this is what you would respond to
this is what it is all about
hear my song
krek-ek

## THE CLEARING

the clearing answers all questions
whether it is the translucent dew
or my transparent desire

a terminal twig has the impetus to die
yet hangs on
in determined hesitation

if asked what is perfection
one might suggest the full tree
with a nest of robins

or the white orchid
or the sense of invisible breath
or the imponderable red dawn

there is a hidden force
moving from every direction
it has been here since the beginning

not silence not persistent noise
but climbing through every life
approaching to the very end

## IN THE WOODS

hemlocks are flawed neighbors
both moss and heat move uncomfortably
Evening Grosbeaks are in the astonishment

violence of humans is far away
if we knew what to look for
it would chill us

rain breaks silence
it fidgets with red turning leaves
whispering by slow degrees

longing never comes from here
there is weakness in limbs
burdened by rushing winds

winged-seed
in emptiness
unopened

from the night of maples
fleeing out
darkening

## QUICKENING

in the advent of first breath
eternal
immense as a familiar thunder

we are immersed in love
its signature is inside us
constellations blinking

## SENSING IN THE DARKNESS

the hush-silence before dawn
when snow muffles this world
a part of an awakening
to experience what is happening

gentle flakes
free-falling in slowness

light is powderpuff blue

silence is ripped so we might hear
what we need to hear

crackling passages of light

the awareness of birds
stirring the unseen

## BEYOND SIGHT

there is always some remote landscape beyond sight
light finds
incrementally
some bend of future is still searching to rescue
a loneliness undulating like unkempt promises
that last unexplored area

I do not know where it is

it is there whether I can find it or not
light knows where it is

there are nights
where I fill in the blank sky
my son's name

then the stars shatter

I find pieces after a rainstorm

## OF MOMENTARY BREATHS NONE OF US COULD EVER RECOVER

a chilled draft wafts
from the wilderness of nightmares

we should be hardwired
two heartbeats

not molting
like a mute swan dragging its webbed feet
through the lilies and seaweed
begging for sunlight

our lives are flights of momentary breaths
none of us could ever recover

## WE LIVE WITHIN EXPANDABLE MUSIC

ash-light enters the seed
untouched by shadow
or processed by fireflies

this is how much I love you
a firework of eyelids
on the fringe of silk

a saturation of rivers can't stop
nor a pulverization of darkness
nor light dashing on your face

before you enter a room
as red leaves in fall
explaining the flight of bees

## FALL

what I thought was pink rain
were cherry blossoms

an embassy of sparrows
congregated in the branches

riffling songs
stumbling joy

the world was changing
in quickening seconds

what seemed mystical
was really everyday presence

## FALL MESSAGE

rain contains incidental sounds
the season has left now
light-charcoal clouds
hold forthcoming snow

before you know it
you'll hear spring
opening bright-yellow daffodils
the grape hyacinths
and iris narcissus-type fritillaria

I am writing to tell you this

the sky is bleeding a sunrise
speaking the motion of birds
whispering inside of me
incurable melodies

making and correcting and unmaking
winging this way
separating what is transforming

the fine print of our life
warns it will never be easy

the world is untying life from life
descending the long staircases of light
in solid rain
musical notes hidden in the universe

when morning sky is murderously red
mourning doves
twinge in the deepness

I slip between
the cool bedsheets
touch my wife
to make sure the world is still here

## FIVE UNTITLED SHORT POEMS

*

when snow became blue
silence fell out of the sky
covering a jay

*

we could wait for messages
but this is all we get

a gathering of geese
fly out past this page in life

I stood in the back yard
left behind

but a part of me
follows that calling

*

a hummingbird
desires the moon's nectar
darts and stitches sky

*

cold wind shakes windows
honey smells flood for hours
red shadows hide bees


\*


in the lavender sky
the blood red sun
writes more grief

## COME THROUGH THE WAIST-HIGH FERNS

come to me
the weight of sleep
inside words

luxuriant
a burst of apple blossoms
arching color over haze

consider my heart
summoning you
among many others

my voice lapping
a windmill
slowly twisting

the flesh of air wants more
come to me from any location
no place should be without you

## OBSERVATION

the intense chorus of birds predicts an afternoon storm
their high-pitched explanations
thrust vibrations into leaves

a profound drop in temperature
fetches pellets of sleet
popping on the sidewalk

ice crystals
marbleized as hard as pennies
crack clang rapidly thunk

it arrives
a furious drumroll
all the birds know is coming

unlike birds
we are unprepared
for the consequences

## THE NIGHTINGALE ONLY SINGS AT SUNSET

the nightingale knows every good day
needs a great serenade
intense praise

water lilies settle into ponds
when night pulls its shades
darkening the thickening fronds

blue chicory
close their tiny hearts in the tender field
near the old clump of hickory

all day the earth was saturated with light
you could feel
the way honeysuckle tasted yellowish flight

now is the time to surrender like a monk
coming down a mountain and reeling
from contemplating so hard he is almost drunk

he climbs descending scales
from the nightingale
sleep songs shimmering on water in a pail

before the sun sets
all we need is this moment when the sky pales
to listen where the world will rest

## I DIDN'T KNOW WHAT TO SAY

I wanted to write about the birch trees
near the green stream
gathering speed
down uneven rocks
under the influence of the nonchalant wind
before the stillness
repeated
I miss you

the conversation of birds
in the pine breeze
startling the sensitive ferns
at the stream's edges
going around a corner
into quiet shadows

I miss you
like the green patches of moss
want the birch
for its small colonies of life

I miss you
standing in green shadows
enjoying water and wind
stillness of rocks
edging the stream
with promises

everything important
every conversation happening
rushes and streams
to be with you

I am not certain what to say
but now that I've written this
it is the unsayable being spoken

**NOW**

the past is seamlessly behind us
it cannot budge it can only fade
ripples behind a boat

time is not elliptical
lavender on the far field never lasts
but death is forever and lacks color

the future is eternal but war is present
while love eclipses
remembrance is changeable

for all this stillness there are ants on peonies
that know they must act while they can
before the moment passes

**FOLDING**

she folds laundry
still smelling soap
lilies and lilacs

dovetailing
into memory
of life's wear and tear

gracefully old
a trace of a life well-spent
a sachet of memories

## PADDLING

I can guide my spirit
towards the withheld

if I reach out
I can touch the skirt of the island

I can paddle over pine reflections
as sirens sing like loons

I do not need a boat
I can simply walk upon the waters

## HOW TO KNOW LOVE # 2

riddles of birds keep dipping in
and out of light
in a hurry to get somewhere

flickers of horse
race across fields
searching for the end of fences

oaks practice silence
rivers never tell where they are going
rain subsides

this is how we search for each other
slurring into each other's arms
sighs of roses

## MAPLE LEAF WINGS

paper thin
maple seeds loosen
helicopter down
twisting
trusting they will make it
but only a few will survive
this first cruel lesson

when someone finds men
in their secret foxholes
more will be wiped out
shifting battle lines

luck changes
with wind or daylight
random as raindrops

one must be vigilant

when dying enters the equation
hope twists into hopelessness
into arbitrariness
then we become
the slow ones who go about
drifting through life
as if living was unimportant

## EVENTUALLY

the dampened wood with the half-melted snow
and the slow sure way icicles drop a piece of loss
softens in the dead mulching leaves
searching for any permanence

even a stone drifts in time
cool springs lose some chill
when heat is transferred from your touch
none of this eternal

loss can only last so long
parts as a silent bird
eventually there will be half the stars
rain can only cool the world off a little

## THE WAY

the body does not let go of its journey
it resists each undecided step
along the way

stopping to observe
if it is time to leave or stay
or to be allowed to follow the calling

the body resists or receives
it cannot resolve its dilemma
until it accepts all of its mistakes

all those times it should have hesitated
the body forgives
relaxes

if you need to let go then go
if you need to stay then stay
nothing will stand in your way

## WHEN MERCY IS ABSENT

light exits our body
a small quake of flickering wind

everything we knew becomes false
we are not shrouded in blessings
nor are we beckoned

we pass through a blue wall in the sky

pain always gathers towards the end

our bodies look back to where we've been
where we are headed
threshing out our pain

we lose so much
it hardly seems to matter

## **AUTUMN CLOUDS**

*Painting by Eric Sloane*
*"the sky was created for pure beholding" — Eric Sloane*

over thirty different variations of blue
as a storm gangs-up
are ready to double-down on dropping
hail or retribution

temperature changes the white-washed barn
faded grey-blue
as a grizzled old man's unshaven chin
and blisters the paint like worn knuckles

weather-beaten to a pulp
down for the count
taken one too many upper-cut blows
the hill grass flattens powder-blue

the shortness of breath
is in the stacked hay bales
like blue-faced sugar cubes
the hard-set winds stir harsh and icy

slat shutters rattle-clack
weather-vane shifts its weight
gates curve with low pressure
autumn is bending the rules

## THE CLEARING

the clearing answers all questions
whether it is the translucent dew
or my transparent desire

a terminal twig has the impetus to die
yet hangs on
in determined hesitation

if asked what is perfection
one might suggest the full tree
with a nest of robins

or the white orchid
or the sense of invisible breath
or the imponderable red dawn

there is a hidden force
moving from every direction
it has been here since the beginning

not silence not persistent noise
but climbing through every life
approaches to the very end

## NOT ONLY THE EXTRAORDINARY ARE ENTERING THE DREAM WORLD

*"... but others not less extraordinary who step lightly in to the dream life, refusing to leave"*
— Jim Harrison, Returning to Earth

we come to the dream world
as a tormented river blistering with dead fish

we traveled a doubt-filled pebble lane
recanting every step and this
is where it has taken us

*taken* is the perfect word for what has happened

we were yanked out of place
from the life we had ignored
to a place where you cannot avoid what you see
and you keep promising
*this is not real*

it is real and tangible
and we cheapen it by our presence

we came to this dream world all splintery
with our dark and forbidding edges

yet all love reaches a certain velocity
like a tree split perfectly in half by lightning
or like a bird losing flight
when colliding on a clear window
or milkweed sending seeds wherever they can go

## ACKNOWLEDGMENTS

These poems appeared in the following magazines, anthologies, chapbooks, full-length collection, and some have been changed over time. I want to thank all of those editors and publishers.

*13 Myna Birds*: "Miracles are a Dime a Dozen"

*2018 Parks & Points* (National Parks website): "Camping"

*30 Poets*: "Spring"

*About Place*: "The Absence of a Lake"

*The Bamboo Hut*: "Five Untitled Short Poems"

*Big City Lit*: "From the Closeness of Oak, Where Dark Holds Breath"

*Black Poppy Review*: "When Mercy Is Absent"

*Broadkill River Review*: "Revitalizing"

*California Quarterly*: "Folding"

*Califragile*: "Rain Patterns"

*Comstock Review*: "Rowing"

*The Drought Anthology*: "Heat Index Breaks the Temperature Gauge"

*Flint Hills Review*: "Teenagers Hiking in a Forest"

*Furious Gazelle*: "Lost"

*Galway Review*: "When Light Reaches Us"

*Halcyon Review*: "In the Woods," "Quickening"

*Hummingbird*: "Argument"

*Loch Raven Review*: "Paddling"

*Montuck Review*: "Clear Cut"

*New Mexico Review*: "At Mountain Crest"

*New Verse News*: "It Is Drizzling Heat"

*Origami Poetry Project*: "At the End of Day," "Nighttime"

*Panoply*: "Exploring the Mountain Range"

*Peacock Journal*: "Dry Spell," "Of Momentary Breaths None of Us Could Ever Recover"

*Poetry Matters Project* (Contest Finalist): "An Exaltation of Larks"

*Poetry Quarterly*: "Beyond Sight"

*Poppy Road Review*: "Defeated," "Eventually"

*Prairie Wolf*: "Forest"

*Red Wolf Journal*: "Van Gogh's Starry Night"

*Shelia-Na-Gig*: "The Way"

*SNReview*: "In the High Hills"

*Verse-Virtual*: "Day Lilies," "Fall"

*The Whirlwind Review*: "Clear for Miles and Miles," "Morning"

*Wild Word*: "Encounter," "Sensing in the Darkness"

*Zingara Poetry Picks*: "Releasing the Dark Landscape," "There is Darkness to the Water"

"Above the Spring Tâf," "Below the Beech, Above the Tâf" appeared in the full-length collection, *Dylan Thomas and the Writing Shed* (FutureCycle Press, 2017)

"Autumn Clouds," "Extreme Heat," "Not Only the Extraordinary are Entering the Dream World," "Walking Hill Slopes," "What I Want," "The Wire Fence Holding Back the World" appeared in *The Wire Fence Holding Back the World*, winner of the *2016 Turtle Island Quarterly Editor's Choice Chapbook Award* (Flowstone Press, 2016)

"The Bird Count" appeared in *The Circle is Never Broken* (Raw Dog Press, 1980)

"The Clearing," "Some Things You Can Never Repair," "Why Darkness Whimpers" appeared in the chaplet, *Some Things You Can Never Repair* (Black Poppy, 2017)

"Come Through the Waist-High Ferns" appeared in the chapbook, *Nasturtiums in Snow Understand Green is Coming* (Foothills Press, 2018)

"Dawn," "The Nightingale Only Sings at Sunset" appeared in the anthology, *Tranquility* (A Kind of Hurricane Press, 2016)

"The Day They Stole the Water," "Water Music" appeared in the *Water Anthology*, (Beatlick Press, 2017)

"The Glass-Faced Deer of Boonville, New York" appeared in the three-author chapbook collection, under the section *Transition* (Writers Resource Center of Toledo, 1985)

"How to Find Love," "How to Find Love #2," "Twenty Reasons" appeared in *You Enter, and it All Falls Apart: 19 Love Poems* (Flutter Press, 2018)

"The Lilac Bushes and the Forest-Tent Caterpillars," "Silk Worms" appeared in the chapbook, *Swimming in the Ladle of Stars* (Kattywomus Press, 2014)

"Longing is Like the Seed" appeared in the full-length collection, *The Heart Knows, Simply, what it Needs* (Aldrich Press, 2012)

"Maple Leaf Wings," "Now" appeared in the mini-chapbook *Vanished into the Impossible* (Origami Poetry Project, 2016)

"March" appeared in the full-length collection, "*Searching for What is Not There,*" winner of the *2013 Wild Earth Ecology Award* (Hiraeth Press, 2013)

"The Organ Mountain Range" appeared in the anthology, *Dingleberry Peak: An Anthology of Organ Mountains Desert Peaks Poems* (2015)

"Pacific Treefrog" appeared in the chapbook, *Falling in and Out of Love* (Pudding House Publications, 2005)

"Six Love Poems" appeared in the min-chapbook, *Six Love Poems* (Origami Poetry Project, 2020)

"Snake River" appeared in the chapbook, *How to Find Peace* (Pudding House Publications, 2012)

"Some Things You Can Never Repair" appeared in the mini-chapbook, *Some Things You Can Never Repair* (Black Poppy Review, 2003)

"Speaking the Language of Deer" appeared in the chapbook, *Why Women Are a Ribbon Around a Bomb* (The Last Automat Press, 2011)

**ABOUT THE AUTHOR**

Martin Willitts Jr, edits the *Comstock Review*, and judges New York State Fair Poetry Contest. He has won numerous awards, including the 2014 Dylan Thomas International Poetry Contest, the 2018 Stephen A. DiBiase Poetry Prize, and the 2020 Editor's Choice for *Rattle*'s Ekphrastic Challenge. His 25 chapbooks include *The Wire Fence Holding Back the World* (Flowstone Press, 2017), winner of the *Turtle Island Quarterly* Editor's Choice Award. His 22 full-length collections include *The Temporary World* (Blue Light Press, 2019), winner of the Blue Light Award.

www.ingramcontent.com/pod-product-compliance
Lightning Source LLC
Chambersburg PA
CBHW041128110526
44592CB00020B/2730